SUPER TRUCKS

**LONDON, NEW YORK,
MELBOURNE, MUNICH, AND DELHI**

DK PUBLISHING
Project Editor Ashwin Khurana
Senior Art Editor Jim Green
Designers Hoa Luc, Mary Sandberg
Managing Editor Linda Esposito
Managing Art Editor Diane Peyton Jones

Category Publisher Laura Buller
Senior Production Controller Gemma Sharpe
Production Editor Adam Stoneham
Picture Researcher Liz Moore
DK Picture Librarian Romaine Werblow

Jacket Editor Manisha Majithia
Jacket Designer Laura Brim
Jacket Design Development Manager Amanda Lunn

Publishing Director Jonathan Metcalf
Associate Publishing Director Liz Wheeler
Art Director Phil Ormerod

DK INDIA
Art Editors Neha Sharma, Nidhi Mehra
Design Interns Shreya Sadhan, Shruti Singhal
Senior Art Editor Chhaya Sajwan
Managing Art Editor Arunesh Talapatra

Project Editor Suparna Sengupta
Managing Editor Pakshalika Jayaprakash

DTP Designers Neeraj Bhatia, Tanveer Zaidi

DTP Manager Balwant Singh
Production Manager Pankaj Sharma

First American Edition, 2013
Published in the United States by
DK Publishing, 375 Hudson Street, New York, New York 10014

Copyright © 2013 Dorling Kindersley Limited
2 4 6 8 10 12 14 16 17 15 13 11 9 7 6 5 4 3 1
001—187003—2/13

A catalog record for this book is available from the Library of Congress.

ISBN 978-1-4654-0248-6

DK books are available at special discounts when purchased in bulk for sales
promotions, premiums, fund-raising, or educational use. For details, contact: DK
Publishing Special Markets, 375 Hudson Street, New York, New York 10014 or
SpecialSales@dk.com.

Color reproduction by Alta Image, UK

Printed and bound in China by Hung Hing

**Discover more at
www.dk.com**

SUPER TRUCKS

WRITTEN BY
Clive Gifford

44 FUN AND GAMES

Let's load up!

Trucks come in all shapes and sizes, from small pickups and mini trucks to giant ultra-class haulers that are too heavy for roads and work in mines or on construction sites. All trucks are powered by some kind of engine, and transport loads from place to place. In this book, you can read about a huge variety of trucks that are built to perform lots of different jobs. Buckle up!

LIGHT

Pickup Light truck with an open cargo bed used for dozens of different tasks, on and off the road

Forklift Vehicle with blades—called forks—to raise, lower, and carry goods around a warehouse, factory, or port

Small flatbed truck Smaller vehicle with a flat cargo area—called a bed—behind the driver's cab

MEDIUM

Garbage truck Vehicle that carries waste from homes, offices, and stores to a dump or recycling center

Tow truck Vehicle that can lift and pull broken-down or stuck vehicles to safety, or to a garage for repairs

Recreational vehicle (RV) Truck that provides a home on wheels, containing beds, kitchen facilities, and toilets

HEAVY

Articulated truck Large cab is connected to one or more cargo trailers by pivot joints that allow them to go around corners

Ultra-class hauler Giant, powerful dump truck capable of carrying enormous loads of rock or soil

Tanker Vehicle that carries large quantities of liquid—such as milk or gasoline—in sealed tanks

EARLY TRUCKS

In the early 18th century steam wagons did exist, but the first motorized truck in history was not built until 1896.

Nicolas Cugnot from France built this artillery gun–towing tractor powered by steam in 1769; it ran for only 10–15 minutes at a time.

The **first truck** powered by an engine that burned gasoline was created in 1896 by German engineer Gottlieb Daimler.

This small truck from 1920 was **based on a Model T Ford car** with a flat bed at the back for carrying loads.

Mini truck Tiny truck that has a small, energy-efficient engine and scoots small amounts of cargo around busy streets

Mini dumper Vehicle with a hopper (a tippable box) used for landscaping, farming, and on smaller building sites

Van Small truck with a high, enclosed body often used for carrying packages, food, and other deliveries around towns

Crawler Truck that runs on continuous tracks and is capable of traveling over rough or icy ground

Ambulance Lifesaving vehicle that brings medical aid to emergencies and carries patients to hospitals

WOW!
More than four million **heavy trucks** were produced in factories around the world in 2011. More than three times as many light trucks were also built!

Concrete mixer Truck that carries concrete or cement in a drum, which turns to keep the material mixed and runny

Transporter Truck that tows a trailer carrying one or more cars, trucks, or other motor vehicles

Giant crane truck Vehicle equipped with a large crane boom that can reach high, or lift up heavy loads

Every day, all over the world, millions of trucks hit the road. Trucks deliver everything from apples to diapers, cars to chocolate bars. They help fight fires, tow aircraft, recover broken-down vehicles, and lift steel girders. They also take away unwanted garbage, and ferry the injured and sick to hospitals, saving hundreds of lives every day. Meet some of the trucks that never rest, and help make modern life run smoothly.

Hard at work

PICKUPS

Pickups are real workhorses, and are built tough and sturdy to withstand heavy use. These small, light trucks hold the driver and passengers in the front cab, and behind that, an open bed can carry many different loads. They can ferry supplies, crops, building materials, and people across rough ground, roads, trails, and fields. Many are equipped with four-wheel drive so they can drive across extremely rugged terrain.

WOW!
Built in Australia, HSV's Z-series Maloo R8 is the **world's fastest** production pickup truck with a top speed of 168.7 mph (271.5 km/h).

DODGE RAM D3500 LARAMIE
These powerful pickups with styling taken from big rigs have proven popular ever since they were launched by Dodge in the 1990s. The strong steel bed behind the cab can hold loads weighing more than 5,000 lb (2,268 kg).

Hinged metal flap called a tailgate opens downward for easy loading

HOW TO FOUR-WHEEL DRIVE

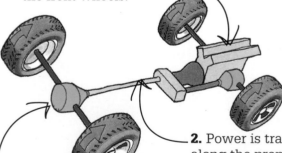

1. The engine generates power, which turns two half shafts that drive the front wheels.

2. Power is transmitted along the propeller shaft to the rear wheels.

3. The rear differential allows the rear wheels to turn at different speeds when traveling around corners.

Load bed made of steel with places to attach ropes and cables

LENGTH 18.7 ft (5.7 m)	**ORIGIN** USA

More than twenty people are hitching a ride on this **Toyota pickup** in Phnom Penh, Cambodia.

A 33 ft (10 m) long model of an *Allosaurus* dinosaur makes an **unusual load** on an old pickup going to California.

Cab seats fully recline so driver and passenger can lie down and sleep

Powerful engine under the hood generates power to turn all four wheels

Ford F-series

The Ford motor company was one of the first to build pickup trucks. Its debut model was based on a Model T Ford car and went on sale in 1925 for $281. Twenty-three years later, the first Ford F-series pickup was launched. Twelve generations of F-series trucks have been built since, with sales of more than 34 million vehicles, making it the world's most popular pickup.

FORD F-47

YEAR 1948
LENGTH 15.7 ft (4.8 m)
FEATURES One-piece windshield, strong suspension, steel bed floor

FORD F-100

YEAR 1953
LENGTH 15.7–17.1 ft (4.8–5.2 m)
FEATURES Redesigned body, wider bench seat, automatic transmission option

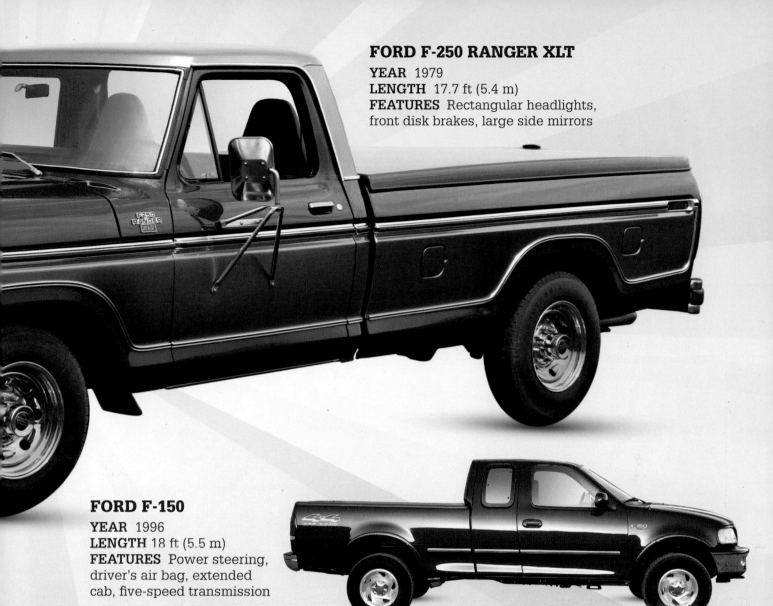

FORD F-250 RANGER XLT

YEAR 1979
LENGTH 17.7 ft (5.4 m)
FEATURES Rectangular headlights, front disk brakes, large side mirrors

FORD F-150

YEAR 1996
LENGTH 18 ft (5.5 m)
FEATURES Power steering, driver's air bag, extended cab, five-speed transmission

FORD F-150 STX

YEAR 2009
LENGTH 18 ft (5.5 m)
FEATURES V8 engine, side air bags, Super Cab seats up to five people

THAT'S AMAZING!

Ford's F-250 Super Chief concept vehicle featured an engine able to run on three different fuels—ethanol, regular gasoline, or hydrogen. It could drive 500 miles (804.6 km) between fuel stops.

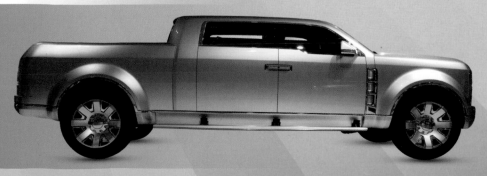

VOLVO A30E

This hefty building-site dump truck hauls large, heavy loads of rock and earth. It can power around construction sites at speeds up to 32.9 mph (53 km/h), and turn tight corners.

Sealed cab allows only filtered air to enter, so the driver's space is dust-free

Hydraulic cylinders and pistons can tilt body to tip out load in just 12 seconds

DUMP TRUCKS

Dump trucks move loose loads, such as sand, rock, coal, snow, and ice from one place to another. They are sometimes known as tippers because their bodies can tilt upward to tip out their load when they reach their destination. Other dump trucks are equipped with hoppers, which tip out loads to the side, or are bottom dumpers releasing their load underneath the truck.

OFFLOADING

This truck **dumps its load** of cut grass in a farm field. Dump trucks on farms can haul soil, fertilizer, animal fodder, and harvested crops.

The bed or hopper can hold up to 31 tons (28 metric tons) of rubble, sand, or other materials

A30E

VOLVO

WOW!
The Michelin 59/80R63 XDR tire used on some of the world's biggest dump trucks is 13.22 ft (4.03 m) tall and weighs **11,680 lb** (5,300 kg).

HOW TO HYDRAULIC RAM

1. The engine provides power to run a pump, which pushes hydraulic fluid through tubes called lines.

3. The piston's top is fixed to the dump truck bed, tilting it up as the piston rises.

2. The fluid enters the cylinder and pushes the piston up with intense force.

LENGTH
33.8 ft
(10.3 m)

ORIGIN
Sweden

15

Lifters and cranes

Many trucks are able to lift up loads and carry them from place to place. Forklift trucks have blades called forks, which slide underneath a load and then raise it up off the ground. Other truck cranes have a large arm called a boom, which extends out from the vehicle. These can lift building materials up high, carry vehicles out of ditches, or raise up technicians to repair overhead cables.

LENGTH	ORIGIN
58.92 ft (17.96 m)	USA

WOW!
A giant truck crane, made by SANY Heavy Industry, has **seven sections** and can extend up to 282.74 ft (86.18 m) in length.

Wide cab glass gives driver a clear view of the road or site ahead

Hand controls and foot pedals help the driver control the crane's movement from inside the cab

WEIGHT LIFTER

This **Hyster E1.75XMS** forklift truck uses two metal forks to raise, lower, and carry boxes around a warehouse.

Crane hook and boom can lift loads of more than 150 tons (136 metric tons)

TEREX DEMAG AC 250-1

This heavy lifter has a crane boom made of separate steel sections, which slide into each other when the truck is on the move, but can slide out to form a crane.

Large turntable that is able to turn to the left and right holds the boom securely in place

HOW TO OUTRIGGERS

1. Hydraulic pistons force the outrigger struts out sideways from the truck's body.

2. Pads extend downward and push down hard on the ground to lift up the truck.

3. The wheels lift off the ground to give the truck a very firm, stable base.

Twelve large rubber wheels are sturdy and can withstand heavy loads

Outriggers are stabilizing posts that support the crane and help keep it from toppling over

17

Fighting fires

Fire! Fire! Wherever a fire occurs, you can rely on fire trucks to get there as quickly as possible. A wide range of trucks have been developed to work in different emergency environments, from forest fires to blazing buildings. The trucks are equipped with all kinds of equipment, including powerful water pumps and hoses, giant ladders, and fire axes.

AIRCRAFT RESCUE
An Oshkosh aircraft rescue vehicle works at Phoenix Sky Harbor Airport. These vehicles are built with sharp acceleration to reach a damaged aircraft quickly. They also have powerful pumps—some can spray more than 2377.6 gallons (9,000 liters) per minute.

FIGHTING FOREST FIRES
This fire truck tanker operates in the countryside, spraying a chemical known as a fire retardant. It helps stop bushes and trees from catching fire, and prevents forest fires from spreading.

ROBOTIC FIREFIGHTER
The future of firefighting may involve robotic trucks tackling a blaze, controlled by humans a safe distance away. This prototype Japanese firefighting truck called Rainbow 5 has a remote-controlled water cannon and a large grabber to move things out of its way.

TO THE RESCUE
A fire truck is parked outside a major fire. Its telescopic ladder is extended so that firefighters can tackle the blaze from above, as well as rescue any victims trapped in the upper stories.

MY STORY:
BEN BEHAN

COUNTRY UK
JOB Firefighter
STATION Bournbrook Fire Station in Birmingham, UK
SERVICE West Midlands Fire Service

Ben's shift starts with a thorough check of his personal protection equipment (PPE)—the gear he has to wear when called out to an emergency. Training and drills ensure that Ben and his colleagues are ready for all situations, such as a recent rescue of an unconscious couple from a burning, smoke-filled 15th-floor apartment.

MCNEILUS HLS GARBAGE TRUCK

Garbage trucks have to make dozens of short journeys and stops between houses to pick up waste, which uses up a lot of fuel. This fleet of trucks in Seattle has been equipped with an energy-saving system that stores energy from regenerative braking to power the truck as it pulls away from one stop to the next.

Solid steel body called a hopper stores waste inside

3017

GVW 49,500

Carbage trucks

What a load of garbage! Households in Britain, the United States, Canada, and Germany generate more than 992 lb (450 kg) of waste per person every year. Most of this solid waste has to be transported away from the home to recycling centers or dump sites by garbage trucks. These are built to be sturdy and strong and can empty a full load of garbage rapidly.

WASTE HAULER

This **front loader** garbage truck grips dumpster bins and lifts them up and over the truck cab to empty the garbage into its rear waste container.

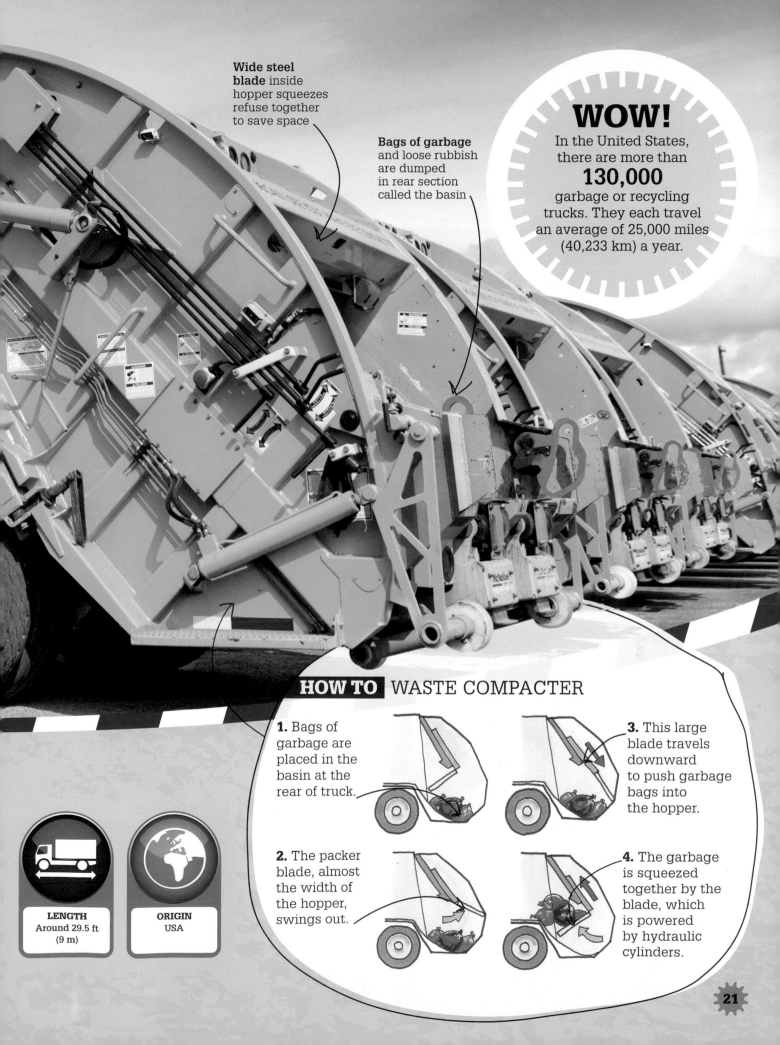

Wide steel blade inside hopper squeezes refuse together to save space

Bags of garbage and loose rubbish are dumped in rear section called the basin

WOW!
In the United States, there are more than **130,000** garbage or recycling trucks. They each travel an average of 25,000 miles (40,233 km) a year.

HOW TO WASTE COMPACTER

1. Bags of garbage are placed in the basin at the rear of truck.

2. The packer blade, almost the width of the hopper, swings out.

3. This large blade travels downward to push garbage bags into the hopper.

4. The garbage is squeezed together by the blade, which is powered by hydraulic cylinders.

LENGTH
Around 29.5 ft (9 m)

ORIGIN
USA

Articulated trucks

Heavy haulers! Most of the longer trucks you see on the roads are articulated. This means that they have a special pivoting joint that enables long trucks to turn around corners smoothly. The articulated joint also allows different trailers to be hitched behind the truck, so that after one trailer is delivered the truck can be hitched to a different trailer to haul a new load.

LOGGING RIG
This powerful truck is hauling a trailer loaded with logs cut from a forest, and is on its way to a sawmill. The trailer features high supports to hold the stacked logs.

VIEW FROM ABOVE
You can see how the articulated joint allows a truck to turn, pulling the frame of an empty trailer behind it. The trailer can be loaded with a container.

FIFTH WHEEL
This large disk accepts a rod called a kingpin that is attached to the trailer. The kingpin can turn while held in the fifth wheel's slot, which allows the truck and trailer to pivot.

MY STORY:
IOWA 80

COUNTRY USA
FIRST OPENED 1964
OPERATED BY The Moon family
CLAIM TO FAME World's largest single truck stop

Built close to the busy Interstate 80 highway that runs from New Jersey to San Francisco, this giant truck stop has parking for 800 trucks and their trailers. Truckers stop for fuel, repairs, or a break. In 48 years, Iowa 80 has served more than 64 million customers, and serves two million cups of coffee every year!

CAB TO TRAILER
These curled hoses and cables supply electrical power from the truck to the trailer's lights and other electrical parts. They also supply air to power the pneumatic brakes.

BIG RIGS

Watch out, coming through! The heaviest tractor unit (the part that pulls the trailer) used in an articulated truck is known as a big rig. Big rigs are equipped with extremely powerful engines, which can haul massive, fully-loaded trailers—or pairs of trailers. In the United States, the heaviest regular trucks and trailers can weigh up to 80,000 lb (36,287 kg)—anything heavier requires special permission. Here are some truck-makers who have become famous for their powerful and reliable big rigs.

KENWORTH TRUCK COMPANY
FOUNDED 1939
ORIGIN USA
HEADQUARTERS Kirkland, Washington
BIGGEST RIGS Kenworth C540 and W900

PETERBILT MOTORS COMPANY

FOUNDED 1939
ORIGIN USA
HEADQUARTERS Denton, Texas
BIGGEST RIG Peterbilt 397

THAT'S AMAZING!

The Scania R730 has one of the biggest, most powerful engines of any big rig. A typical family car's engine is 0.4–0.6 gallons (1.4–2.4 liters) in size. The R730's engine is 4.3 gallons (16.4 liters) and delivers 730 horsepower.

DAF

FOUNDED 1928
ORIGIN The Netherlands
HEADQUARTERS Eindhoven
BIGGEST RIG DAF XF105

MACK TRUCKS

FOUNDED 1900
ORIGIN USA
HEADQUARTERS Greensboro, North Carolina
BIGGEST RIGS Mack Titan and M100SX

VOLVO

FOUNDED 1928
ORIGIN Sweden
HEADQUARTERS Gothenburg
BIGGEST RIG Volvo FH16

Mini haulers

Some trucks are built small and narrow so they can scoot through tight spaces in crowded cities to deliver small but important cargo. Mini trucks are usually less than 9.8 ft (3 m) long and lightweight, so they can be powered by small, fuel-efficient engines. Japanese *kei* were among the first mini trucks, but today thousands of mini trucks are also built in India, Italy, and South Korea.

Small two-stroke engine is very economical

LENGTH
8.8 ft
(2.7 m)

ORIGIN
Italy

HOW TO TWO-STROKE ENGINE

1. Fuel and air ports are closed and opened by a moving piston.

2. The piston moves up the cylinder and squeezes the fuel and air together, which are then burned.

3. Expanding gases in the cylinder push piston down, allowing new fuel into cylinder.

4. Waste gases leave cylinder through an opening called the exhaust port.

LITTLE WORKER

A **Japanese _kei_ truck** is equipped with a tall box trailer to hold more cargo, which it can deliver through the busy streets of Tokyo, Japan.

WOW!

One mini truck has been turned into a tiny **11 ft (3.4 m)** long fire truck operating in Shibukawa City, Japan.

Small cargo bed is 4.6 ft (1.42 m) long and 4 ft (1.2 m) wide, and can carry up to 441 lb (200 kg) of cargo

PIAGGIO APE 50

This three-wheeled mini truck is just 4.13 ft (1.26 m) wide, perfect for delivering loads along alleyways behind stores and restaurants. Drivers can choose whether to steer using a steering wheel or handlebars.

Fuel tank holds just 2.6 gallons (10 liters) of gas

CRAWLER

Track attack! Crawler trucks are used on farms, building sites, beaches, and snow-covered ground. They run on continuous tracks (a loop of rubber or metal links) that are turned around by sets of wheels and rollers driven by the truck's engine. Crawlers tend to move at slower speeds than wheeled vehicles, but they are often better over soft or rough ground. They spread the weight of the truck over a much larger area than wheels, stopping the truck from sinking into the ground.

LENGTH	ORIGIN
18 ft (5.48 m)	UK

TALUS MB-H

This crawler tows a heavy lifeboat down to the sea on the northwest coast of England. Its tracks are angled upward at the front to climb obstructions that are in the truck's way.

Driver's seat can turn 180 degrees in the cab to face the direction it's traveling in

Tracks enable truck to tow a lifeboat weighing more than 11 tons (10 metric tons) at a speed of up to 7 mph (11 km/h)

M3

B188 GAW

WOW!

Three rows of four continuous tracks, each 12 ft (3.8 m) wide, support the giant Bagger 288 mining vehicle, which weighs **44,092 tons** (40,000 metric tons).

MAKING TRACKS

This **Caterpillar excavator** uses its tracks to support its great weight as it moves across the mud at a construction site.

The powerful tracks on a **Tucker Sno-Cat** provide grip as it travels across Ross Island, just off the coast of Antarctica.

LYTHAM ST. ANNES LIFEBOAT

HOW TO CONTINUOUS TRACKS

1. Powered by the engine, the front wheel turns and grips the track, pulling the crawler forward.

2. The track travels under the road wheels, gripping the ground and propelling the crawler truck forward.

3. The idler wheel and the return rollers along the top keep the track in shape.

4. The rear wheel is also powered by the engine and can reverse the crawler.

HOW TO | STRADDLE CARRIER

1. A large container-long device called a spreader locks on top of the container.

2. The straddle carrier can move along the dock via its sets of wheels.

3. The driver in the cab positions the straddle carrier in the right place and raises or lowers the container.

4. The container truck underneath the crane receives a container on its flatbed trailer.

Steel container is 20 ft (6.09 m) long and can hold up to 31.1 tons (28.2 metric tons) of cargo inside

Container trucks

Millions of large, standard-sized steel boxes called containers are traveling around the world as you read this. These containers hold all kinds of products, from toys to food, and because they are of the same size, cranes and vehicles can handle them easily. Container trucks haul containers from docks or railroad depots on roads to be unloaded at their final destination.

High cab position gives driver a clear view of road ahead

DAF XF105

This big, reliable, long-distance container truck hauls two standard steel containers from a port to their destination. Each container was loaded by crane onto the truck's flatbed trailer, then secured, before setting off.

CARGO CARRIER

A large port handles huge numbers of containers. The **Chinese port of Shanghai** handles 26 million every year.

A truck delivers a container to a port to be **shipped overseas**. Containers are designed to be stacked on top of each other to save space.

Powerful headlights protected by clear Lexan plastic, which is almost unbreakable

LENGTH Around 52.5 ft (16 m)

ORIGIN The Netherlands

LONG-HAUL TRUCKER

Long-distance truckers drive vehicles that cross countries or continents. They must concentrate all the time to drive safely, since the long hours can be tiring, and being away from home for long periods can be difficult. Still, many truckers love the feel of the open road.

Grille channels air over the radiator inside, cooling the engine

WEIGHING THE TRUCK
Truckers have their trucks weighed on giant scales known as truck scales. These make sure that a truck isn't overloaded and is light enough to cross a bridge.

TAKING A NAP
Not all trucks have built-in beds, so this trucker from India has come up with an ingenious solution. He's rigged up a bed hanging from cables slung underneath his truck.

Vertical exhaust stacks release waste gases from the engine

Tinted windshield reduces the sun's glare on the driver's eyes

THE JOURNEY AHEAD

A big rig hauls a box trailer down a highway. The extended cab of the tractor unit contains a bed for sleeping in and simple cooking facilities so the driver can live in his or her vehicle.

MY STORY: ALLEN SMITH

COUNTRY USA

JOB Long-haul truck driver for more than 30 years

CLAIM TO FAME Wrote the book *The Truth About Trucking*

Allen is an experienced long-distance trucker. He has hauled loads across Canada and the 48 continental U.S. states, traveling almost 4 million miles (6.44 million km) in the process. Truckers like Allen use their radios to talk to other truckers, warning each other of traffic or road problems ahead on routes.

LOADING TRUCKS

A forklift truck loads a trailer. A trucker may have a "no touch" policy, meaning he doesn't load or unload his truck but must make sure the load is secure throughout the journey.

Tankers

Tankers carry large quantities of liquids from place to place. These liquids can be chemicals, paints, foodstuffs (such as milk or liquid chocolate), or gases, which are put under pressure so that they turn into liquid. Large numbers of tankers ferry gasoline from oil refineries to gas stations.

Cab is made of aluminum, reinforced with steel, and has wide windshield for clear views ahead

M2 106 FREIGHTLINER

This six-wheeled tanker can carry a range of liquids in its giant tank. The truck features a sloping hood and two sets of rearview mirrors, which are mounted on the hood and window, so the driver gets good views behind when reversing.

Engine generates up to 350 horsepower to pull truck, which can weigh as much as 55,206 lb (25,041 kg)

LENGTH	ORIGIN
8.9 ft (2.7 m)	USA

A tanker carrying **liquid chemicals** pulls into a plant in Poland that makes polyester fibers used in clothing.

A tanker hauls two trailers of milk from New Zealand dairy farms. The **refrigerated tanks** keep the milk cool.

Access hatches on top of large aluminum tank can be opened to check liquids inside

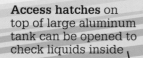

WOW!

The first drive-in gas station opened on Baurn Boulevard in Pittsburgh in 1913. It sold **only 30 gallons** (114 liters) of fuel on its first day.

HOW TO GAS STATION

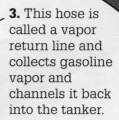

1. The hose is attached to the valve on the truck's tank, which can hold thousands of gallons of gas.

3. This hose is called a vapor return line and collects gasoline vapor and channels it back into the tanker.

2. The gas is pumped from the tanker into the underground fuel tanks of a gas station.

CONCRETE MIXERS

Let's get building! Concrete is the world's most common building material, forming the base and walls of many structures, as well as paths and roads. A mixer truck keeps its load of concrete in prime condition by turning it around in a large drum before delivery.

MERCEDES AXOR 3535K/51

This concrete mixer can weigh more than 33 tons (30 metric tons) when its large drum is full of heavy concrete. This immense weight is supported by two sets of wheels at the rear of the mixer.

WOW!
The Ancient Romans used concrete more than **2,000 years ago**. Today, around 2.2 tons (2 metric tons) of concrete is made each year for every person on the planet.

Large engine runs on diesel fuel and sits below the driver's cab

LENGTH
29.9 ft
(9.1 m)

ORIGIN
Germany

Drum is turned by powerful motors to keep concrete mixed

The concrete from this mixer travels down the **delivery chute** into the bucket of an excavator.

This truck pumps concrete up a **long tube called a boom** to deliver it to the top of a building.

HOW TO MIX CONCRETE

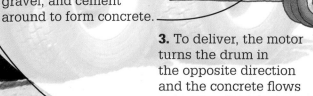

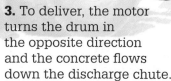

1. The curved metal vanes help mix the materials together and keep them from settling and hardening.

2. The mixer's motor rotates the large drum, which moves the sand, gravel, and cement around to form concrete.

3. To deliver, the motor turns the drum in the opposite direction and the concrete flows down the discharge chute.

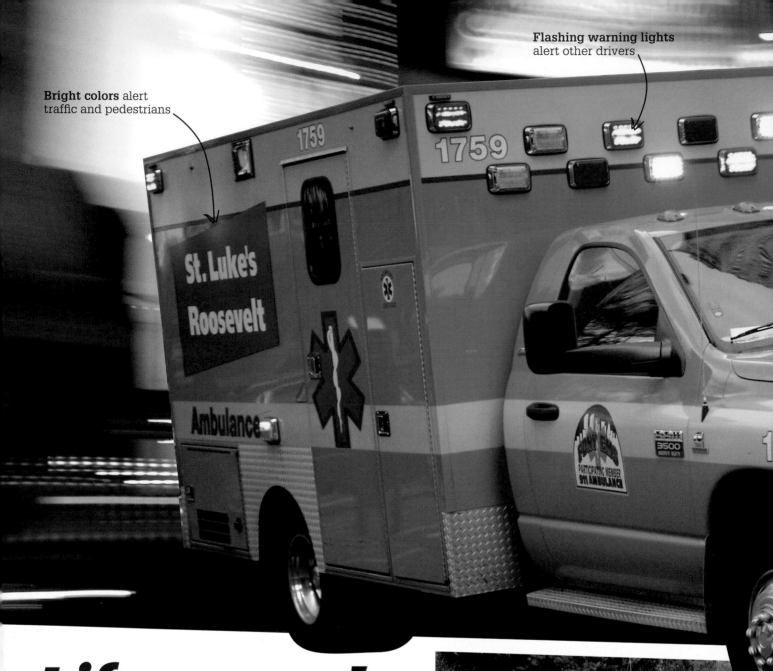

Bright colors alert traffic and pedestrians

Flashing warning lights alert other drivers

1759

1759

St. Luke's Roosevelt

Ambulance

3500

Lifesavers!

Lights flash, sirens wail, the traffic ahead clears and an ambulance goes flying by. Every second counts in an emergency so ambulances respond rapidly to emergency calls, weaving through traffic to reach the scene, and taking seriously ill and injured people to the hospital as quickly as possible.

ALL-TERRAIN AMBULANCE
This off-road ambulance is built on a Nissan Patrol four-wheel-drive vehicle and attends accidents at rally races. All-terrain ambulances are used to cross rough ground to reach ill or injured people.

Powerful 1.6-gallon (6-liter) engine produces 300 horsepower, more than twice the amount of a family car

MY STORY: BRIAN KELLETT

COUNTRY UK
BORN 1971
JOB Ambulance driver
CLAIM TO FAME Well-known blogger who wrote for TV

After working as a nurse, Brian trained to become an ambulance technician, learning how to navigate and drive an ambulance quickly but safely around city streets. Brian wrote a blog about his experiences, which became two books and a TV series.

RESPONDING TO THE CALL

An ambulance from the St. Luke's-Roosevelt Hospital Center races through the streets of New York. It is one of 10 St. Luke's ambulances that respond to 27,000 calls per year, and deliver 20,000 patients to hospital emergency rooms.

INSIDE AN AMBULANCE

An ambulance is like a mini emergency room on wheels. It features bench seats, a wheeled stretcher (a gurney), a breathing apparatus, and a range of lifesaving medical machines, drugs, and treatments.

HISTORIC LIFESAVER

A 1910 motor ambulance is driven in London, England. Compared to the smooth ride offered today, a journey in an early ambulance with little suspension over cobbled streets must have been bumpy and sometimes painful!

EVO 4 TRANSPORTER

The British-built Evo 4 transporter carries up to 11 new cars via a system of tilting ramps and decks so that one car tucks under another to make the most of space.

Rear half of transporter runs on six wheels, three on each side

TRANSPORTERS

Cars and vans are built by the millions by auto manufacturers every year. These have to be transported from factories to showrooms and dealers. Long-distance transportation is undertaken by ships and trains, but for the last part of the journey, on roads, new vehicles are usually carried secured firmly on the decks of transporter trucks.

LENGTH
61.5 ft
(18.75 m)

ORIGIN
UK

Angled ramps tilt cars, allowing more vehicles to fit onto transporter

Steel posts support weight of the top vehicle deck

FREEMANS

FREEMANS

01933 356213

FREEMANS

Trailer linked to truck cab and engine by fifth wheel allows vehicle to turn corners smoothly

HOW TO LOAD A TRANSPORTER

3. Straps fed through the car's wheels are tightened to lock it into place on the transporter.

2. Hydraulic pistons raise or lower parts of the transporter's deck.

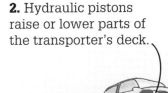

1. Cars are loaded on via ramps in the reverse order they need to be delivered.

DOUBLE DECKER

A **NASCAR vehicle** is loaded into a two-story transporter, which holds cars at the top. The workshop, kitchen, and storage areas are below.

Tow trucks and tugs

Every day, thousands of people thank a tow truck driver for getting them out of difficulty. Tow trucks can recover broken-down cars, buses, and other trucks, towing them to a garage for repairs. Trucks that tow entire aircraft are known as tugs. They tow and maneuver aircraft on the ground to their correct terminal or gate at an airport for loading, unloading, and refueling.

FORD MODEL A 1929

ORIGIN USA
JOB Small breakdown truck
MAXIMUM TOWABLE WEIGHT
2.75 tons (2.5 metric tons)

DAF XF

ORIGIN The Netherlands
JOB Breakdown and recovery truck
MAXIMUM TOWABLE WEIGHT
220.4 tons (200 metric tons)

THAT'S AMAZING!

Some airport tugs possess serious pulling power. They need it for towing the world's largest airliner, the Airbus A380, which, fully loaded, can weigh more than 617.2 tons (560 metric tons).

VOLKSWAGEN T5

ORIGIN Germany
JOB Breakdown van
MAXIMUM TOWABLE WEIGHT
2.2 tons (2 metric tons)

SCHOPF F210

ORIGIN Germany
JOB Airliner tug
MAXIMUM TOWABLE WEIGHT
308.6 tons (280 metric tons)

JUNGHEINRICH EZS 570

ORIGIN Germany
JOB Airport baggage truck
MAXIMUM TOWABLE WEIGHT
7.7 tons (7 metric tons)

Fun and games

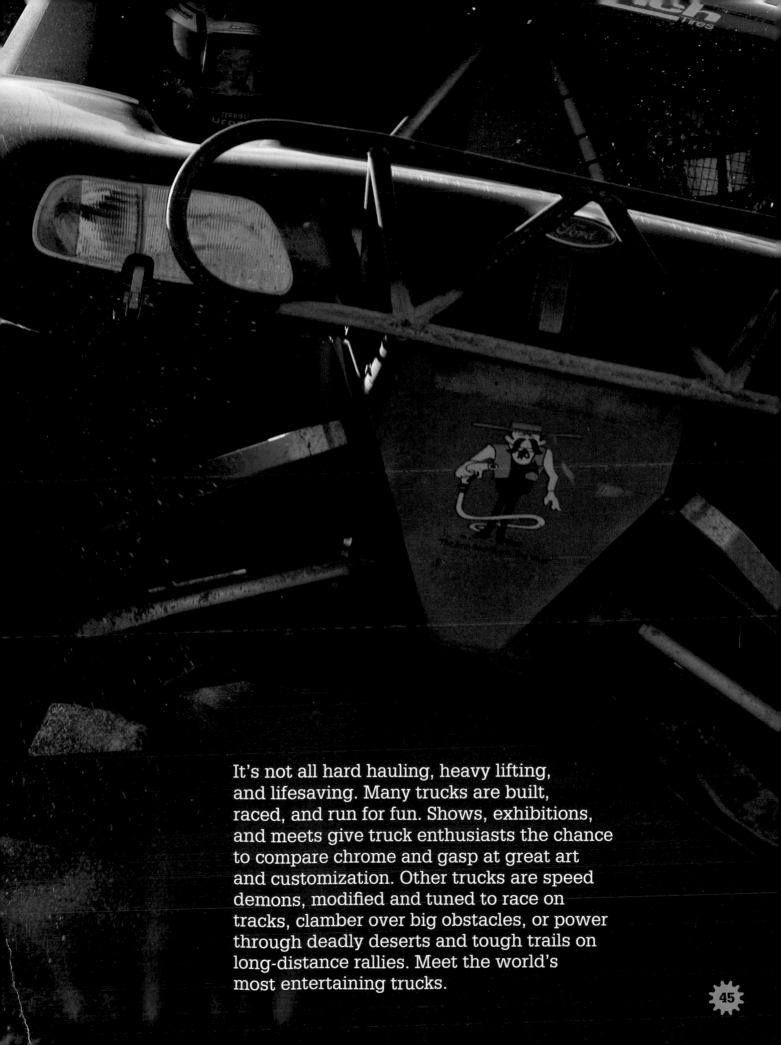

It's not all hard hauling, heavy lifting, and lifesaving. Many trucks are built, raced, and run for fun. Shows, exhibitions, and meets give truck enthusiasts the chance to compare chrome and gasp at great art and customization. Other trucks are speed demons, modified and tuned to race on tracks, clamber over big obstacles, or power through deadly deserts and tough trails on long-distance rallies. Meet the world's most entertaining trucks.

STEAM WAGON

Hisssss! The first trucks were powered by steam made in a boiler heated by coal burned in a furnace. Steam wagons started operating in the 19th century and were used to haul loads—mainly in the UK—until the 1930s, by which time diesel- and gasoline-engine trucks were kings of the road. Some steam wagons, however, remain in top condition and are popular attractions at steam rallies and truck shows.

SUPER SENTINEL

Built in 1930 to transport flour—and bought by the British navy in 1970—this Super Sentinel has a vertical boiler that needed 12 gallons (45.5 liters) of water every minute to run at a top speed of around 20 mph (32 km/h).

HOW TO STEAM ENGINE

1. Water is heated in a large boiler and becomes steam, which is piped to the engine cylinder.

2. Steam pushes a piston inside the cylinder, which a crankshaft then converts into turning movement.

3. The turning movement powers the chain to drive the rear wheels of the steam wagon.

This **Foden D** steam truck has a horizontally mounted boiler and wheels made of steel covered in a layer of solid rubber.

This **Clayton & Shuttleworth** steam wagon was built more than 90 years ago; it has been restored to run at steam fairs.

Canopy used in the past to cover spare bags of coal for use as fuel

Bed of truck can hold a load of up to 6.6 tons (6 metric tons)

LENGTH
23 ft
(7 m)

ORIGIN
UK

Gleaming chrome exhaust stack channels exhaust gases out from the engine

120509

Landstar
RANGER

USDOT 241572
VN 433997

CUSTOMIZED RIGS

Stand out from the crowd. Many truck owners and drivers take great pride in their vehicle, keeping them in perfect condition and displaying them at truck festivals and shows. Many customize their trucks, adding chrome parts and airbrushing intricate and colorful designs and images on their outsides, as well as tricking up the trucks' interiors.

FANCY FLEET

Got enough time and paint? Then how about customizing an entire fleet of trucks? These rigs from French trucking company Jean Rouillon Transport have paintings of famous racing and movie stars on their cabs.

ON SHOW

Many truck customizers can't wait to exhibit their handiwork at truck shows. This 1960 Chevy pickup, complete with airbrushed flames on its hood, is being exhibited at a show in Fairbanks, Alaska.

FLY LIKE AN EAGLE

A Landstar Ranger heavy hauler has been given a patriotic makeover, painted with part of the U.S. flag fluttering behind a bald eagle—the national bird of the United States. It can take hundreds of hours of work to get a truck to look this good.

RESTORED RIG

Some old trucks, like this 1950s Chevrolet 3100 pickup, are given a new lease on life as they are restored back to new condition, given a sparkling paint job and plenty of brand-new chrome bumpers and trim.

Truck decorations

Look into a rearview mirror and see what truck is looming up behind you. Most truck manufacturers feature their company logo or design on the front of their vehicles, making them recognizable in an instant. In the past, these logos were sometimes very elaborate sculptures.

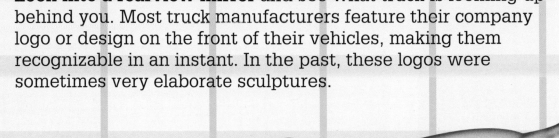

MACK TRUCKS

ORIGIN USA
FOUNDED 1900
SYMBOL FACT These trucks were nicknamed "bulldogs" during World War I

DODGE

ORIGIN USA
FOUNDED 1900
SYMBOL FACT Mountain ram chosen since it is quick and sure-footed over rough ground

TOYOTA

ORIGIN Japan
FOUNDED 1937
SYMBOL FACT Linking ovals represent Toyota's products, customers, and technology

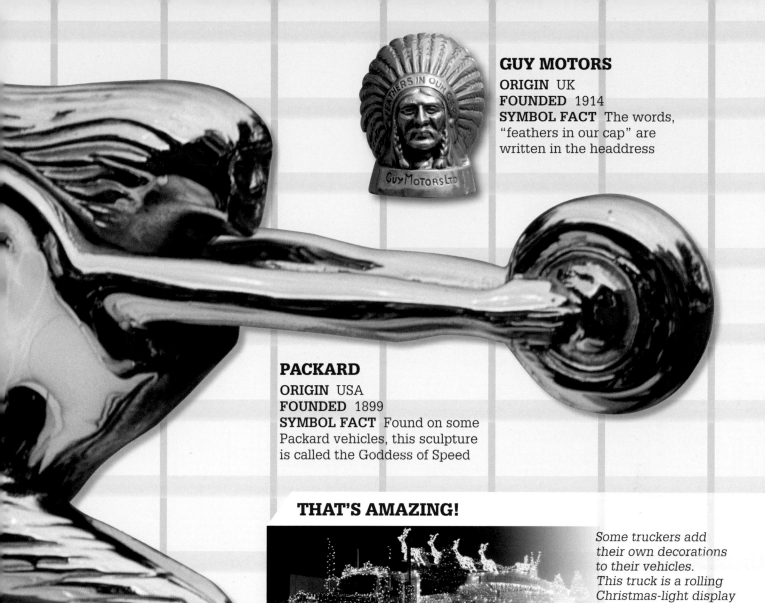

GUY MOTORS

ORIGIN UK
FOUNDED 1914
SYMBOL FACT The words, "feathers in our cap" are written in the headdress

PACKARD

ORIGIN USA
FOUNDED 1899
SYMBOL FACT Found on some Packard vehicles, this sculpture is called the Goddess of Speed

THAT'S AMAZING!

Some truckers add their own decorations to their vehicles. This truck is a rolling Christmas-light display with lit up Christmas trees and Santa Claus in a sleigh pulled by reindeer.

FORD

ORIGIN USA
FOUNDED 1903
SYMBOL FACT Famous Ford script created in 1909, with blue background added in 1927

MERCEDES-BENZ

ORIGIN Germany
FOUNDED 1926
SYMBOL FACT Star with three points was originally the logo for Daimler cars

SCANIA

ORIGIN Sweden
FOUNDED 1900
SYMBOL FACT Features mythical creature with head of eagle and body of lion

RACING TRUCKS

Start your engines! High performance pickup trucks compete in NASCAR's Camping World Truck Series. This competition features 22 exciting races held on many of North America's most famous tracks. Trucks made by Chevrolet, Toyota, Dodge, and Ford race close together, thrilling fans with lots of overtaking and fast action. The trucks have no doors so drivers enter and exit through the window.

WOW!

At the 2010 Mountain Dew 250 race in Alabama, Kyle Busch won the race in 1 hour 48 minutes by a margin of **0.002 seconds**, ahead of Aric Almirola.

CHEVROLET SILVERADO

Kevin Harvick drives this speedy vehicle on his way to winning the 2012 Kroger 250 in Virginia. His truck uses a large rear wing called a spoiler to deflect air downward and help grip the track.

Timothy Peters in truck number 17 runs close behind John King (in number 7). This technique is called drafting and helps save fuel.

Roll cage made of steel tubes welded together protects driver if vehicle crashes and tumbles over

HOW TO PIT STOP

3. A tire carrier takes away the old worn tires and supplies the tire changer with new tires.

1. The jack man uses a hydraulic jack to raise the wheels on one side off the ground.

2. A tire changer uses an air-powered wrench to remove the five nuts holding the wheel.

650-horsepower engine under locked-down hood propels truck to a top speed of more than 170 mph (273 km/h)

Brake air intake channels air onto the wheel's disk brakes to help cool them down

LENGTH
17.3 ft
(5.29 m)

ORIGIN
USA

Homes on wheels

Home sweet home... on wheels. Recreational vehicles (RVs) provide people with a place to live on the road. More than eight million households in North America own an RV. These vehicles are designed carefully and ingeniously to pack in as many household features as possible—from beds and toilets to stoves and refrigerators—so that people can live on the road. The electrical devices inside an RV are usually powered by an onboard electricity generator.

LENGTH
44.91 ft
(13.69 m)

ORIGIN
USA

WOW!
One of the first RVs was the 1910 **Touring Landau** driven by a chauffeur. It included a fold-down bed, a sink, and a pot for a toilet.

Powered awning canopies can slide out to provide shade when parked

HOW TO GENERATOR

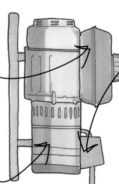

1. Fuel, such as diesel, from fuel tank (yellow) burns inside the engine (gray) to generate power, turning a shaft.

2. Inside the generator, the shaft turns a rotor, which induces an electric current.

3. The electric current is transformed into the correct voltage for powering the RV's electric devices, such as room lighting, TVs, refrigerators, stoves, and air-conditioning.

NEWMAR ESSEX 2012

A luxury mini hotel on wheels, this giant RV is packed with home comforts inside, from a power shower and home theater system, to a king-size bed, an ice maker, toilets, and even a doorbell!

This small **1967 Mini Wildgoose camper van** squeezed in a double bed and dining table for four people.

A **classic Volkswagen Type 2 bus** from the 1960s has a split windshield, sliding side door, and removable seats.

Broad, one-piece glass windshield tinted to reduce glare from the Sun, allowing the driver to view road ahead

Large side mirrors give the driver a good view behind the RV

Essex

E 8 8 e x

Motor homes

Recreational vehicles (RVs) first became popular more than 90 years ago in the United States as more and more people wanted to tour the country's national parks. Now, these homes on wheels—complete with kitchens, bathrooms, and beds—are popular worldwide. They come in all shapes and sizes, from smaller camper vans to monster luxury motor homes with PCs, power showers, and home theaters.

VOLKSWAGEN TYPE 2 1972

ORIGIN Germany
LENGTH 14.8 ft (4.5 m)
FEATURES Pop-up roof, sink and faucets, foldout table

TRAIL AIRE

ORIGIN USA
LENGTH 33 ft (10.05 m)
FEATURES Two LCD TVs, rearview camera, refrigerator-freezer, stove

THAT'S AMAZING!

Driving off a campsite to buy some groceries or travel through narrow city streets can be tricky in a giant RV. So Travel Supreme's giant A Class RV contains a garage large enough to hold a two-seater Smart Car.

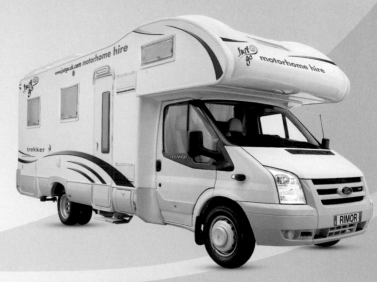

FLEETWOOD PROVIDENCE 2005

ORIGIN USA
LENGTH 39 ft (11.9 m)
FEATURES Powered pull-out awning,
DVD home theater system, massive
fuel tank holding 90 gallons (341 liters)

RIMOR TREKKER

ORIGIN Italy
LENGTH 23.6 ft (7.2 m)
FEATURES Gas central heating,
freezer, bed over cab, locker for
four bicycles

MARCHI MOBILE ELEMMENT PALAZZO

ORIGIN Austria
LENGTH 40 ft (12.2 m)
FEATURES Pop-out living room and roof terrace,
bar, working fireplace, under-floor heating

Desert racers

Blasting across deserts and tough terrain, some trucks take part in the Dakar Rally—the ultimate long-distance race. First held in Europe and Africa, it now occurs in South America and features trucks, cars, and motorcycles racing over difficult ground. Trucks need to be built tough and reliable to race 4,970–6,214 miles (8,000–10,000 km) in just over two weeks.

Cab containing driver and codriver is reinforced with a strong frame of steel tubes known as a roll cage

IVECO TRAKKER EVOLUTION II

The Trakker truck is a powerhouse with a large fuel tank holding 184.9 gallons (700 liters). Its giant 12,900cc engine enables the truck to reach speeds of 99 mph (160 km/h), even though it weighs 20,944 lb (9,500 kg).

Powerful xenon headlights with two pairs of high-beam halogen lights above them light up the route ahead

WOW!
Vladimir Chagin, driving Kamaz trucks, is the Dakar Rally's **most successful competitor**, having won a record seven times.

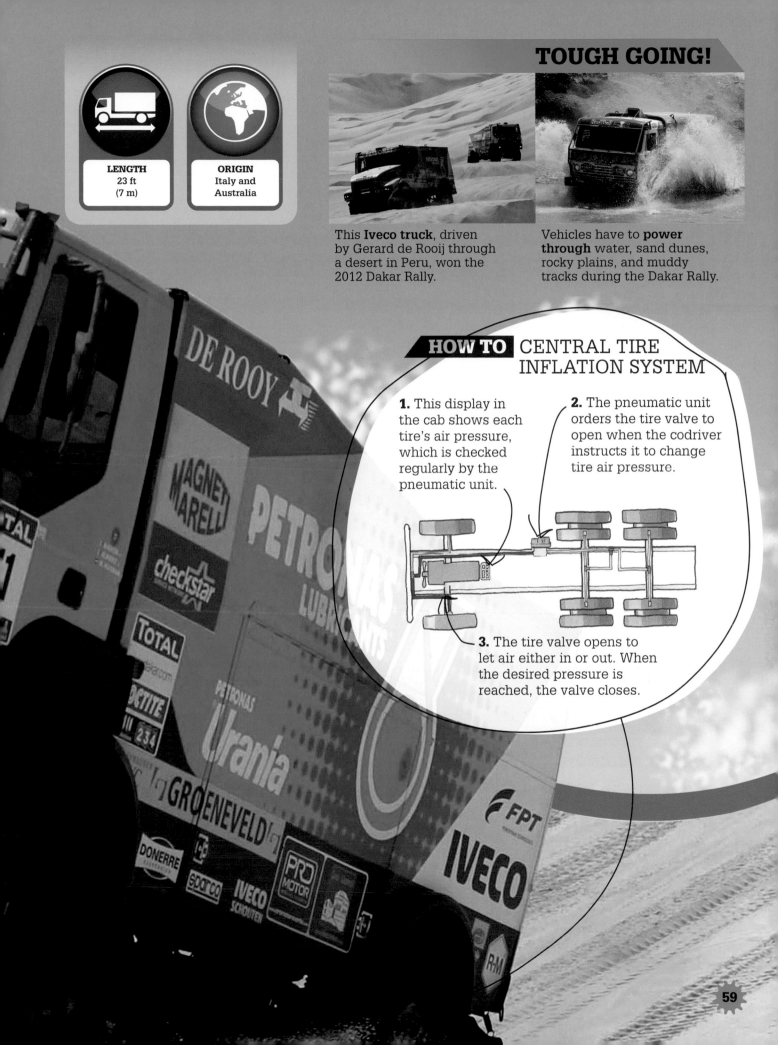

LENGTH
23 ft
(7 m)

ORIGIN
Italy and
Australia

This **Iveco truck**, driven by Gerard de Rooij through a desert in Peru, won the 2012 Dakar Rally.

Vehicles have to **power through** water, sand dunes, rocky plains, and muddy tracks during the Dakar Rally.

HOW TO CENTRAL TIRE INFLATION SYSTEM

1. This display in the cab shows each tire's air pressure, which is checked regularly by the pneumatic unit.

2. The pneumatic unit orders the tire valve to open when the codriver instructs it to change tire air pressure.

3. The tire valve opens to let air either in or out. When the desired pressure is reached, the valve closes.

Dekotora

Turn up the lights! In Japan, when it comes to customizing their trucks, some people really go for it. Dekotora, meaning decorated trucks, are packed full of modifications, many costing thousands of dollars. The trucks gleam with added chrome features, stainless steel panels, dozens of lights, and other colorful decorations. Many are paraded at truck rallies and shows, but some are no longer allowed on roads since their incredibly bright lighting would dazzle other drivers.

MY STORY:
TAKASHI KATO

COUNTRY Japan

TRUCK Peterbilt 377

CLAIM TO FAME Dekotora customizer known for his stunning designs

Kato bought an American Peterbilt 377 truck in 1995 and has spent more than $200,000 turning it into a stunning dekotora vehicle complete with paintings of Native Americans on the side and large external speakers. Kato travels to shows throughout Japan with his truck, and is a member of Japan's largest dekotora club, the *Utamaro-Kai*, with more than 800 members.

LIGHTS OUT
Some dekotora have so many lights that their generators can only power them for a short time. Otherwise, the generator would get too hot and might break down.

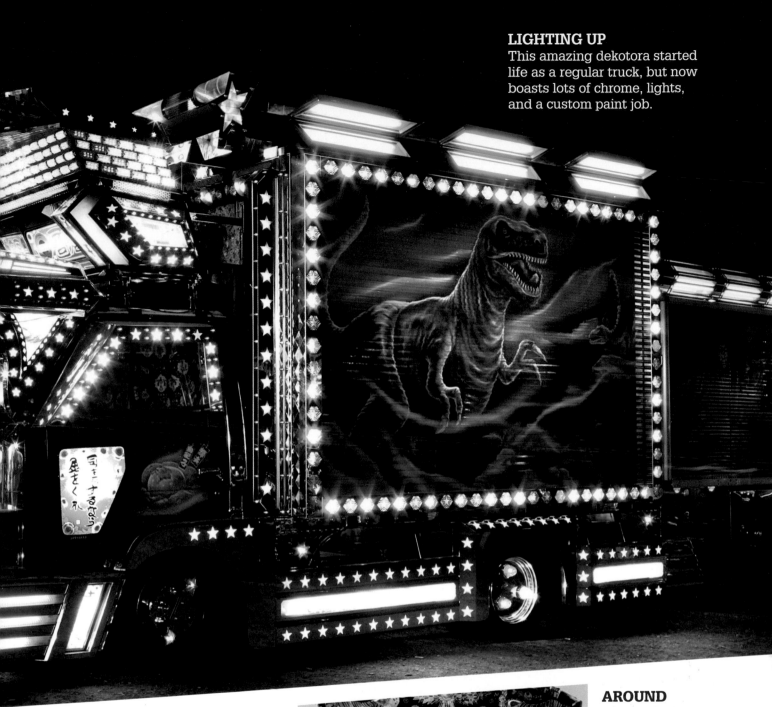

LIGHTING UP
This amazing dekotora started life as a regular truck, but now boasts lots of chrome, lights, and a custom paint job.

A BIT OF BLING

A chandelier hangs from the ceiling of this blinged-up truck cab covered with lights. A programmable computer controls the sequence in which the lights flash and shine, creating an amazing show.

AROUND THE WORLD
Japan is not the only country where drivers trick out their trucks. In Pakistan, many trucks are highly decorated with a large wooden crown called a taj, above the truck cab.

AVENGER
ENGINE TYPE Chevrolet
POWER 1850 hp
WEIGHT 9,500 lb (4,309 kg)
TIRE DIAMETER 66 in (168 cm)

MONSTER TRUCKS

Meet the monsters. These pickups or similar vehicles are equipped with gigantic wheels and tires, and have powerful engines and suspension systems. The result can be mayhem as they perform stunts, take daredevil leaps off ramps, or race against each other, riding over and crushing wrecked cars and other obstacles. Entertaining fans is the name of the game.

GRAVE DIGGER
ENGINE TYPE Merlin
POWER 1500 hp
WEIGHT around 10,000 lb (4,536 kg)
TIRE DIAMETER 66 in (168 cm)

BIGFOOT 5

ENGINE TYPE 460 CI
POWER 1500 hp
WEIGHT around 28,000 lb (12,700 kg)
TIRE DIAMETER 120 in (305 cm)

RAMINATOR

ENGINE TYPE Hemi
POWER 200 hp
WEIGHT 10,300 lb (4,672 kg)
TIRE DIAMETER 66 in (168 cm)

OBSESSION

ENGINE TYPE Merlin
POWER 1500 hp
WEIGHT around 9,500 lb (4,309 kg)
TIRE DIAMETER 66 in (168 cm)

Extreme machines

Some trucks take it to the limit. They may be the biggest, baddest haulers around, capable of carrying a giant spacecraft or hundreds of tons of rock in a single journey. Others operate in the most treacherous conditions imaginable, such as navigating the icy cold wastes of Antarctica, roaring across dry desert roads, or breaking records on red-hot drag racing strips. Amazingly, there are trucks that travel through water or even drive themselves. Welcome to the world of trucking's most extreme machines.

TRIPLE JET TRUCK

Shockwave is a 1985 Peterbilt truck cab that has been given the ultimate high-speed makeover. Its three J34-48 turbojet engines generate around 30,000 horsepower of thrust, enough to take it to speeds past 330 mph (531 km/h). Extra fuel is injected into the back of the jet engines to shoot 50 ft (15 m) long flames out the back.

HOW TO TURBOJET ENGINES

Spoiler helps generate downforce to keep the truck gripping the track

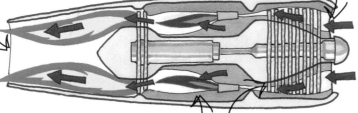

4. The mixture produces large amounts of hot gases, which expand rapidly out of the jet engine's rear exhaust, thrusting the truck forward.

1. The air is sucked into the front of the engine through holes called inlets.

3. The high-pressure air is mixed with fuel injected into the combustion chamber. The mixture is set on fire and burns fiercely.

2. In the compressor, bladed fans turn and squeeze the air together, increasing its pressure.

Jet power

Fire it up! Most trucks are powered by internal combustion engines, but jet trucks are different. They harness the awesome, eye-popping power of jet engines—normally found in military fighter planes—for serious acceleration and speed. When it comes to jet trucks, American Les Shockley is the undoubted king. His Shockwave truck, powered by three jet engines, is the world's fastest, and has reached a world record speed of 376 mph (605 km/h).

Exhaust stack billows flames to wow spectators as fuel is injected and set on fire inside it

FRICTIONATOR

This powerful truck screams down a track. The **Ford F650** pickup truck has been fitted with a single General Electric J85 jet engine, which gives it a staggering 7,000 horsepower.

WOW!
Jet trucks are fuel hogs. The greedy Shockwave can use up to **400 gallons** (1,514 liters) of fuel for every mile (1.6 km) that it runs.

LENGTH
Around 28 ft
(8.5 m)

ORIGIN
USA

ROAD TRAINS

Now that's a truck! In Australia, South America, and some other parts of the world, massive tractor units tow not one but two or more hefty trailers, often over long distances. These trucks need seriously powerful engines to haul such a heavy load, as well as extra fuel tanks because they may have to travel hundreds of miles between stops.

Snorkels channel air into the engine—they are tall to avoid the dirt and dust nearer to the ground

HOW TO DOLLY

1. This small-wheeled trailer called a dolly is attached to the back of the first trailer.

3. The kingpin slots into the fifth wheel, joining the second trailer to the first.

2. The fifth wheel on top of the dolly has a slot that can accept a post called a kingpin.

MACK TITAN ROAD TRAIN

This road train operates in Australia. It features a beefy Titan truck made by Mack, which tows four giant trailers holding coal. Each trailer is connected to another by flexible joints, so that the road train can maneuver around bends and corners.

Additional fuel tanks hold up to 713 gallons (2,700 liters) of fuel

WOW!
A Mack truck pulled the longest-ever road train of 112 trailers, measuring **4,836.9 ft** (1,474.3 m) in length in 2006.

This **Kenworth C509** truck's hoppers are filled with salt before the road train carries them away.

The powerful **Kenworth T909** can pull trailers loaded with a variety of things, including grain, livestock, and mining material.

LENGTH
29.1 ft (8.9 m) tractor unit only

ORIGIN
USA for use in Australia

Bull bars at front push or deflect bushes, fallen trees, and other obstructions out of the truck's path

MACK

KW • 8027

CUTTING EDGE

The problem of moving this wide wooden house has been solved by cutting it in two! Each half of the house is carried by a truck to its new location where it will be fitted together again.

PREFAB HAULING

A truck hauls several prefabricated vacation homes on a long trailer. These small homes are built and assembled in a factory and then transported as a whole to their destination.

House movers

Moving doesn't have to mean changing houses. With the cost of building new properties rising and many people wanting to preserve older wooden and clapboard houses, the building itself can be moved to a new location. Sometimes, this involves a whole home being raised and placed on the back of a giant flatbed trailer and towed by a truck with serious pulling power.

HOME ON THE ROAD

This wide load hogs the whole highway as an entire house is moved in New Mexico. A single Mack truck working in a low gear pulls the house slowly to its new destination.

ARCTIC ACCOMMODATION
Buildings can be built in cities and then transported by truck to isolated areas. These crew quarters for oil workers are being hauled by truck through icy northern Alaska.

MY STORY:
MOVING A THEATER

LOCATION Minneapolis
BUILT 1910
MOVED 1999
WEIGHT Around 2,908 tons (2,638 metric tons)
CLAIM TO FAME One of the biggest building moves ever

The historic Shubert Theatre was raised up on 100 powerful hydraulic jacks so that 70 wheeled dollies could support its weight as it was towed by five trucks 1318.8 ft (402 m) to its new location in the same city—a towing task that took 12 days!

Signs on front of truck (and back of trailer) warn other drivers about the wide and long load

Wheeled dollies help support the house's weight and make the load more stable as it travels along

ERSIZE LOAD

LOAD

Ultra-class haulers

Meet the world's biggest dump trucks. Ultra-class haulers are true monster machines able to carry more than 300 tons (272 metric tons). Fully loaded, these beasts are too heavy for the highway, where their great weight would crush the road surface. Instead, they run off-road on the trails of mines and large construction sites where they haul huge loads of rock and earth away.

LENGTH
47.5 ft
(14.45 m)

ORIGIN
USA

Gigantic hopper is big enough to hold two school buses with space to spare

WOW!
Fully fueled and loaded, the 797B weighs a colossal 1,087 tons (0,985 metric tons). That's the same as 90 adult elephants!

395   797B

HOW TO DISK BRAKE

1. The brake lever is pressed and hydraulic fluid flows down the pipe to push the piston.

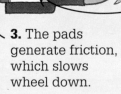

2. The piston presses the brake pads against the disk joined to the wheel.

3. The pads generate friction, which slows wheel down.

4. On the Caterpillar 797B, each wheel has between 10 and 15 disks to greatly increase the braking power.

72

CATERPILLAR 797B

This mighty truck is 32 ft (9.75 m) wide, can carry 380 tons (345 metric tons) of rock in a single journey, and return to the mine face ready for another load at a top speed of 42 mph (68 km/h).

A driver stands in front of his **Euclid Hitachi** truck, which moves rock at the Marigold Gold Mine in Nevada.

Built in Belarus, the **Belaz 75601** is 23.69 ft (7.22 m) tall and powered by a 3,800 horsepower engine.

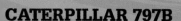

Long steel ladders reach air-conditioned driver's cab, which seats two people and stands more than 16.4 ft (5 m) above the ground

Six giant tires are each 14 ft (4.28 m) in diameter, and weigh 11,684.5 lb (5,300 kg)

Moving giant trucks

Ultra-class haulers are monstrous machines. They are far too big and heavy to run on regular roads, so how are they transported from the factories where they're made to their places of work? Sometimes, these giant trucks are reduced down into small parts, which are then moved by train or ship. Alternatively, other powerful trucks carry them to their final destination.

Chassis and body (without hopper) weighs in at 195.1 tons (177 metric tons

Pair of trucks work hard to pull their load at a modest 18 mph (29 km/h)

MAMMOET

T 282 B

HITCHING A RIDE

This Liebherr T282B ultra hauler is being transported to a mine in Fort McMurray, Canada. It rides on an extremely long trailer—running on more than 70 wheels—that is pulled by two powerful trucks working their hardest.

Each tire weighs more than 5.5 tons (5 metric tons) and contains enough rubber to produce 600 car tires

T 282 B

ALL IN ONE PIECE

The entire hopper of a giant dump truck is hauled along a road near Johannesburg, South Africa. The road has been cleared for the truck to haul its load, which weighs more than 88.2 tons (80 metric tons).

MACK ON TRACK

In northwestern Australia, this Mack Titan big rig tows a large Haulpak dump truck—complete with a heavy spare tire in the hopper—along a highway.

GOLD DIGGER

Once delivered, tested, and refueled, a giant dump truck can get to work. This truck is being filled with rock containing gold from a large open pit in Ghana, Africa.

MY STORY: DESERT TRUCK TREK

COUNTRY Mongolia
BUILT Illinois
YEAR 2009
CLAIM TO FAME Epic drive by giant dump trucks

After a journey in crates across the United States, the Pacific Ocean, and China, these Caterpillar 793D mining trucks were built at Zamyn-Uud, Mongolia, on the border with China. These massive trucks were then driven for 404 miles (650 km) across mostly empty desert to the Ukhaa Khudag coal mine.

Polar trucks

Some trucks are designed to work in freezing-cold conditions close to the North or South Pole. Polar trucks are used in Antarctica, for example, to ferry people and supplies from airfields and ships to bases and research stations on the icy continent. They are often equipped with special heaters in the driver's cab and under the hood to keep the engine warm and running reliably.

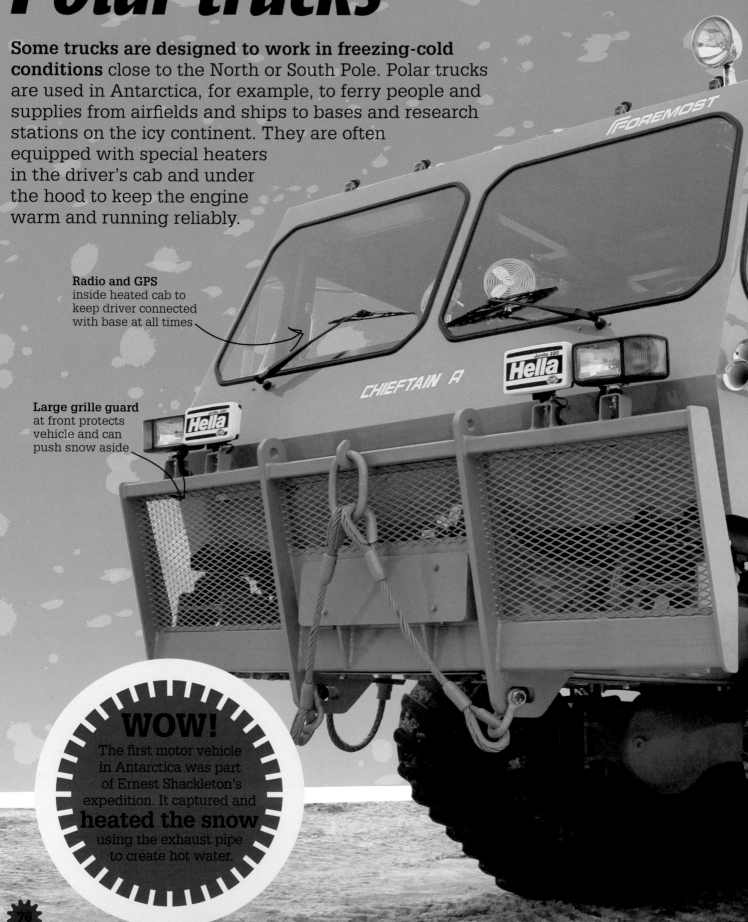

Radio and GPS inside heated cab to keep driver connected with base at all times

Large grille guard at front protects vehicle and can push snow aside

WOW!
The first motor vehicle in Antarctica was part of Ernest Shackleton's expedition. It captured and **heated the snow** using the exhaust pipe to create hot water.

GLOBAL POSITIONING SYSTEM (GPS)

1. A network of satellites in space orbits the Earth.

2. The signals of each satellite's position are sent back to Earth.

3. The GPS receiver receives signals from satellites and calculates its position.

4. The GPS receiver displays truck's location on a digital map shown on its screen.

FOREMOST CHIEFTAIN R

This versatile tracked vehicle can haul loads weighing up to 30,000 lb (13,600 kg) across snow and ice, as well as boggy ground when the snow thaws. The vehicle has eight forward gears and four reverse gears and a top speed of 20 mph (32 km/h).

GET A GRIP!

This **Delta vehicle** contains a cabin able to carry 20 people from an airfield to a research station in Antarctica.

This **Arctic Trucks Toyota** with six-wheel drive can travel more than 2,485 miles (4,000 km) in Antarctica without stopping.

LENGTH
37.7 ft
(11.5 m)

ORIGIN
Canada

Tracks are 34 in (86 cm) wide, made of rubber, and fitted with metal cleats called grousers to dig into the snow and provide grip

Military might

Thousands of trucks are in service with military forces all around the world. They perform crucial roles as military ambulances, troop movers, and weapon carriers. Many transport large amounts of food, equipment, medicine, and other supplies from place to place. Some trucks provide mobile bases from which weapons, such as rockets or missiles, can be launched, or are heavily armored so that they can patrol dangerous areas, protecting the crew inside.

BM21 GRAD

ORIGIN Russia
USE Rocket launcher
FEATURES 40-tube rocket launcher able to fire two rockets per second, top speed of 47 mph (75 km/h)

FOX M93A1

ORIGIN Germany
USES Armored patrol vehicle
FEATURES Chemical sensors to monitor hazards outside, machine gun turret

OSHKOSH HET

ORIGIN USA
USE Tank and heavy
duty transporter
FEATURES Sideways radar to
check for blind spots, powerful
700-horsepower engine

STGO
CAT 3

THAT'S AMAZING!

The Stryker armored off-road
truck has an automatic
firefighting system to put
out fires, a powerful winch
to tow broken-down vehicles,
and can drive more than
25 miles (40 km) with four
of its eight tires flat.

HELEN

H622896

ALBION CX22

ORIGIN UK
USES Transporting troops
and supplies, towing heavy guns
FEATURES 600 mile (960 km) range,
canvas-covered trailer, powered winch
able to lift or tow 8.3 tons (7.5 metric tons)

SMARTRUCK III

ORIGIN USA
USE Mobile command center
FEATURES Remote-controlled
machine gun, night-vision
camera, run-flat tires

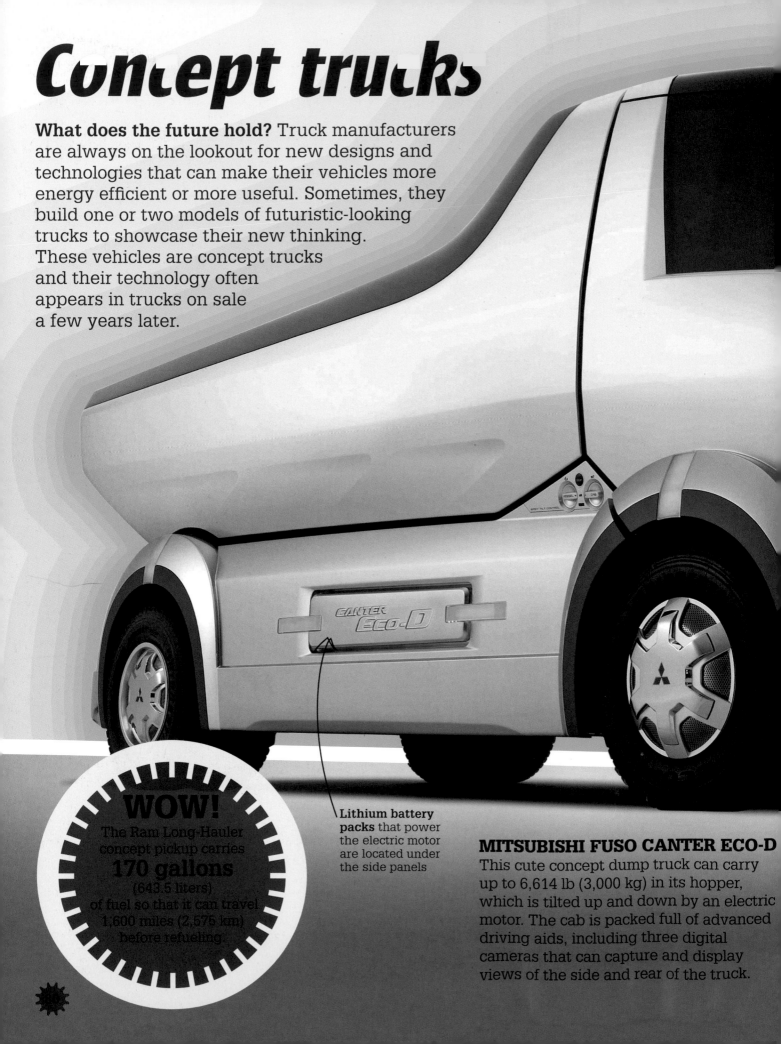

Concept trucks

What does the future hold? Truck manufacturers are always on the lookout for new designs and technologies that can make their vehicles more energy efficient or more useful. Sometimes, they build one or two models of futuristic-looking trucks to showcase their new thinking. These vehicles are concept trucks and their technology often appears in trucks on sale a few years later.

WOW!
The Ram Long-Hauler concept pickup carries **170 gallons** (643.5 liters) of fuel so that it can travel 1,600 miles (2,575 km) before refueling.

Lithium battery packs that power the electric motor are located under the side panels

MITSUBISHI FUSO CANTER ECO-D
This cute concept dump truck can carry up to 6,614 lb (3,000 kg) in its hopper, which is tilted up and down by an electric motor. The cab is packed full of advanced driving aids, including three digital cameras that can capture and display views of the side and rear of the truck.

HOW TO LANE WARNING SYSTEM

3. Small electric motors shake the steering wheel and warning signals sound to wake up the sleepy driver.

2. A digital camera sends images of the road ahead to the lane warning system's control unit, which detects if the truck is drifting out of its lane.

1. Tired truckers can sometimes let their vehicles drift across road lanes, potentially leading to accidents.

FUSO

CANTER Eco-D

Truck body can rise up above its wheels to clear rough ground, or to make tire changing easier

LENGTH
Around 17.7 ft
(5.4 m)

ORIGIN
Japan

FUTURISTIC!

The **Hexawheel** is a 15.7 ft (4.8 m) long concept truck with a unique tilting body to clamber over tall obstacles.

The **Volvo BeeVan** places the driver in the center of the cab and has touch-screen controls and lane warning technology.

An empty crawler weighs 3,000 tons (2,721 metric tons). Unloaded, it has a maximum speed of 2 mph (3.2 km/h) and half that when it's loaded.

The crawler runs on huge, heavy continuous steel tracks that spread out the vehicle's enormous weight. Each of the tracks' links—sometimes called shoes—weighs around 1,984 lb (900 kg).

Shuttle crawler

Meet the 3,000-ton (2,721 metric ton) machine— the shuttle crawler. When in operation, this massive vehicle had the tough task of transporting a space shuttle weighing 2,205 tons (2,000 metric tons) from its assembly building to the launch pad for liftoff. This gigantic 131 ft (40 m) wide truck is powered by 16 electric engines, and is supplied with energy from generators driven by two huge diesel engines.

Driver's cab is dwarfed by rest of vehicle, and there's another cab at the other end of crawler

STOP AND DOCK
The crawler docks the space shuttle with its launch pad. The crawler is a gas guzzler, using 125.7 gallons (475.8 liters) of fuel for every mile (1.6 km) it travels.

GO DISCOVERY!

MY STORY:
SAM DOVE

COUNTRY USA
JOB Electrical engineer
EMPLOYER United Space Alliance
CLAIM TO FAME Shuttle crawler engineer and driver

A former United States Air Force sergeant, Sam worked as an engineer and driver on the shuttle crawler for many years. The cab's controls appear simple—some gauges, a speed controller, and a small go-kart-like steering wheel—but driving the world's heaviest truck requires great patience and accuracy.

Loading platform on the upper deck of the crawler carries the shuttle

Platform is kept perfectly level by 16 hydraulic cylinders

CRAWLING AWAY
The crawler transports the fully loaded *Discovery* space shuttle complete with its giant orange fuel tank to launch pad 39B for its mission to the International Space Station. The 4-mile (6.4 km) journey takes about four hours as the crawler slowly moves along its own road—the crawlerway.

Each corner of transporter is supported and moves on a pair of continuous tracks

Energy savers

Go green! Most trucks run on fuels made from oil, but oil is slowly running out, and engines that burn oil-based fuels create pollution in the air. So some trucks are being built that run partly or completely on alternative fuels, which are more sustainable and create less pollution. Many think that alternative-energy vehicles can help save the planet.

Cargo bed made of aluminum is 4.6 ft (1.4 m) wide and can carry a load weighing up to 1,389 lb (630 kg)

GEM ELXD

Small, quiet electric motors power this eco-friendly electric truck. It can make 50 miles (80.5 km) of local deliveries before its nine battery packs need to be recharged by plugging them in to an electricity supply at home or at a garage.

POWERING UP

LENGTH	ORIGIN
12.1 ft (3.7 m)	USA

This **hybrid truck** is powered by both a regular gasoline engine and electric motors, which help it use less oil-based fuel.

Solar panels on this **Sanyo electric truck** reduce the time its batteries take to recharge, and can power electric bicycles.

Open cabin features large windshield for clear views and seats for a driver and one passenger

HOW TO REGENERATIVE BRAKING

2. The electric wheel motors reverse direction and turn into electricity generators when the truck's brakes are applied.

3. The battery is recharged using electricity generated by the electric wheel motors. The battery can then be used in addition to the engine to help power the truck.

1. This hybrid truck's small, efficient gasoline engine powers the truck with the help of electric wheel motors—on either side of the engine.

PHIBIAN ON LAND
On land, the Phibian is driven like a regular truck with its pair of diesel engines generating a total of 500 horsepower. The truck has a top speed of more than 81 mph (130 km/h).

HUMDINGA
The Humdinga is a smaller amphibious truck, about 21.9 ft (6.7 m) long. It is able to carry loads of up to 1,653 lb (750 kg). As the truck enters the water, its wheels tuck up into the body, which is waterproof and floats.

Gibbs Phibian

Want to go trucking on land and water? A Gibbs truck may be the answer. This high-tech company has started producing small, maneuverable trucks that can travel at high speeds on both water and land. On land, the trucks have four-wheel drive to help them race over all kinds of ground. On water, the wheels tuck up into the truck's body, which becomes a boat hull.

Shallow hull allows Phibian to skim quickly through the water

SEARCH AND RESCUE
Designed to work in difficult terrain, such as swamps and flooded areas, the Humdinga can carry up to seven people. It can be used for search and rescue work, as well as ferrying doctors, medicine, and other vital supplies to emergency scenes.

Body of vehicle mostly made from strong—but light—carbon fiber

MY STORY: ALAN GIBBS

COUNTRY New Zealand
BORN 1939
LIVES London, England
JOB Chief Strategy Officer of Gibbs Technologies

Alan already had decades of success as a businessman when he built his first amphibious vehicle in New Zealand in 1995 so he could go fishing. He formed a company to develop the amphibious Aquada car and the Humdinga and Phibian trucks. Alan says, "Anything you can do with a truck, you can do with these."

www.gibbstech.com

MAKING WAVES
At 30.2 ft (9.2 m) long, the Phibian is the biggest of the Gibbs vehicles and can hold up to 3,307 lb (1,500 kg) of cargo, or 15 people. When on a lake or river, a pair of jet thrusters squirt water out of their rear nozzles to power the Phibian to a speed of up to 31 mph (50 km/h). It takes just five seconds for the truck to make the transition from water mode to land mode.

D.ive.less t.ucks

Lie back and enjoy the ride! Future trucks may not need a driver for part or all of their journey. Some of these vehicles will be remote-controlled from a distance. Others will have a human on board for city driving, but out on long highways the truck will control itself. Driverless trucks may travel one after another in special lanes—known as platooning—using computers and sensors to follow each other closely but safely.

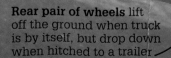

WOW!
In 2010, three driverless vans formed a convoy behind a driven lead van. The convoy traveled **8,077 miles** (13,000 km) from Italy to China.

TAKE A BREAK

This **Komatsu dump truck** working in an Australian mine is driverless! An operator can control the truck remotely using wireless signals.

LENGTH
Statistic not available

ORIGIN
Sweden

Rear pair of wheels lift off the ground when truck is by itself, but drop down when hitched to a trailer

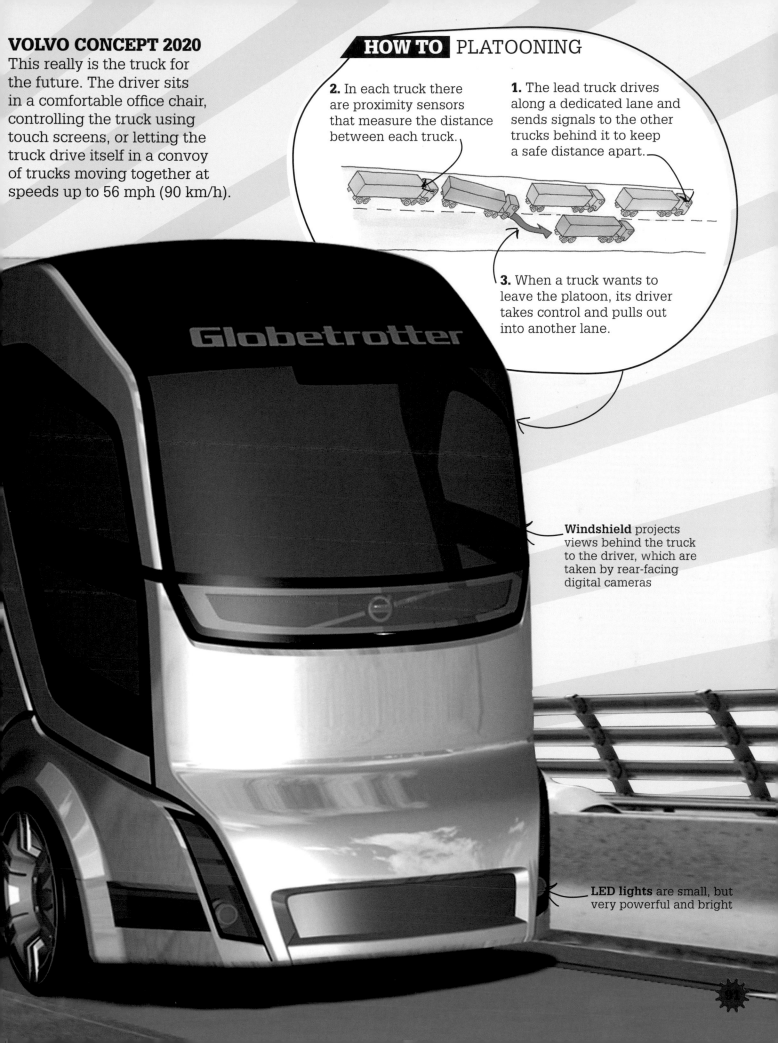

VOLVO CONCEPT 2020

This really is the truck for the future. The driver sits in a comfortable office chair, controlling the truck using touch screens, or letting the truck drive itself in a convoy of trucks moving together at speeds up to 56 mph (90 km/h).

HOW TO PLATOONING

2. In each truck there are proximity sensors that measure the distance between each truck.

1. The lead truck drives along a dedicated lane and sends signals to the other trucks behind it to keep a safe distance apart.

3. When a truck wants to leave the platoon, its driver takes control and pulls out into another lane.

Windshield projects views behind the truck to the driver, which are taken by rear-facing digital cameras

LED lights are small, but very powerful and bright

Glossary

accelerate
To speed up and go faster.

aluminum
A metal that is light in weight and is used for some truck parts.

amphibious
A truck or other vehicle able to travel both on land and in water.

battery
A store of chemicals in a case that supplies electricity when connected to a circuit.

bumper
A metal, rubber, or plastic bar fitted along the front, and sometimes the back, of a truck, to limit damage if it bumps into something.

cab
The part of the truck where the driver sits and controls the vehicle.

chassis
The frame of a truck that supports the vehicle, and to which parts, such as doors and bodywork, are attached.

concept truck
A vehicle built to demonstrate new truck designs or technologies.

customize
To change a vehicle's design, body, and other parts so that it looks different.

diesel
A type of fuel, made from oil, which is used in many truck engines.

disk brakes
A type of brake where pads press against a turning disk to create friction and slow the wheel down.

dolly
A type of wheeled cart that is used to support part of a trailer when it is linked up to a truck or another trailer.

excavator
A vehicle found at building sites that digs holes using a steel bucket attached to a long arm.

exhaust
Tubes that channel waste gases away from a truck's engine and out into the open air.

fifth wheel
The slotted disk that accepts the kingpin to make an articulated joint between a truck and a trailer.

forklift truck
A small truck equipped with bars at the front, which act as a platform to lift and carry goods around a factory, warehouse, or depot.

four-wheel drive
A system where power from the engine is sent to turn both the front and back wheels of a vehicle.

friction
The force that slows movement between two objects that rub together. Brakes create lots of friction to slow a truck down.

fuel
A substance or material that is burned to produce heat or power. In most trucks, gasoline or diesel is used as a fuel.

gears
Toothed wheels that are used in trucks to change the amount of speed or force with which the wheels turn.

generator
A machine that creates electricity for use by electrical devices.

global positioning system (GPS)
A navigation system that uses signals from a group of space satellites to work out a vehicle's position on Earth's surface.

hood
A body panel, usually made of metal, which can open to reveal the truck's engine.

hopper
Large storage area of a truck used for carrying materials between locations, then discharging its load.

horsepower (hp)
A commonly used measure of the power of a truck engine.

hybrid truck
A truck that has both a gasoline engine and another engine or motor, such as an electric motor.

hydraulic piston
A rod that moves in and out of a hydraulic cylinder when pushed by liquids in the cylinder.

NASCAR
Standing for National Association for Stock Car Auto Racing, NASCAR is a very popular type of car and truck racing competition on tracks in North America.

off-road
To travel in a vehicle away from roads and over tracks, trails, or open ground.

outriggers
Bars that extend out from the side of a mobile crane or fire truck and grip the ground to make the vehicle more stable.

piston
A rod-shaped engine part that moves up and down inside an engine cylinder.

pit stop
A break when a vehicle racing on a track leaves the racetrack so that the race team can make repairs, add fuel, or change tires.

pollution
Waste products that reach the air, water, or land, and can do damage to the environment or be harmful to the health of living things.

radiator
A heat-exchanging device designed to help cool a truck's engine.

regenerative braking
A system found in some new trucks in which the forces generated during braking are converted into electrical energy, which recharges a truck's batteries.

road train
A vehicle made up of a powerful truck towing two or more trailers to haul cargo, particularly through isolated parts of the world.

roll cage
A strong frame inside a truck that protects people inside.

solar panel
A device that converts energy from sunlight into electricity.

straddle carrier
A non-road-going vehicle used to stack and move containers, often at ports.

streamlined
A vehicle that is shaped in a way that allows air to flow easily over and around it.

suspension
A system of springs and shock absorbers that help a truck travel smoothly over bumps.

tailgate
The hinged flap at the back of a pickup truck bed that can open and close.

tractor unit
A truck with a driver's cab and a short chassis that is used to haul a trailer.

truck scale
A large machine that weighs a truck and its contents.

ultra-class hauler
A truck used in mines that can carry a load of more than 300 tons (272 metric tons).

Index

Credits

The publisher would like to thank:
Carron Brown for editorial assistance, Jeongeun Park for design assistance, Charlotte Webb for proofreading, Jackie Brind for preparing the index, and Thomas Morse for Photoshop work on the jacket.

All illustrations by Daniel Wright.

The publisher would like to thank the following for their kind permission to reproduce their photographs:

Key: a-above; b-below/bottom; c-center; f-far; l-left; r-right; t-top

4 Alamy Images: Transtock Inc.. **5 Corbis:** Construction Photography (t); George Disario (b). **6 Daimler AG:** (bl). **Charles Dawson:** (c). **John Pittman (www.hawkdog. net/wordpress/):** (cra). **Scania CV AB (publ):** Dan Boman (cl). **Toyota Material Handling UK:** photo of Toyota Traigo HT (ca). **7 Alamy Images:** Ken Walsh (tr). **Corbis:** Martyn Goddard (tc); John Turner (tl). **Daimler AG:** (cra). **Foremost Industries LP:** (clb). **Archivio Piaggio:** (cla). **Scania CV AB (publ):** Göran Wink (br). **Volvo Truck Corporation:** (bc). **8–9 Corbis:** Construction Photography. **10–11 Corbis:** Car Culture. **11 Corbis:** Louie Psihoyos (tr). **Getty Images:** AFP (tc). **12 Alamy Images:** Performance Image (cl, b). **12-13 Alamy Images:** Performance Image (t). **13 Alamy Images:** Drive Images (cb). **Corbis:** Car Culture (ca, b). **14 Alamy Images:** Jim Parkin (b). **14–15 Alamy Images:** Robert Clayton. **16–17 Alamy Images:** RJH_Catalog. **17 Getty Images:** Bloomberg (tl). **18 Corbis:** George Hall (c). **Getty Images:** (cb). **Press Association Images:** AP Photo / Tsugufumi Matsumoto (bc). **18–19 Corbis:** Darren Greenwood / Design Pics. **19 West Midlands Fire Service:** Aaron Manning (c). **20 Alamy Images:** ZUMA Wire Service (b). **20–21 SuperStock:** Spaces Images. **22 Corbis:** Tom Grill (br). **22–23 Alamy Images:** imagebroker. **SuperStock:** Glow Images, inc. (bl). **23 Getty Images:** Walter Hodges (b). **Iowa 80 Group, Inc.:** (c). **24 Alamy Images:** Ivor Toms (b). **24–25 Alamy Images:** Furlong Photography. **25 Alamy Images:** Justin Kase zsixz (br); Rohan Phillips (bl). **DAF Trucks N.V.:** (cr). **Scania CV AB (publ):** Göran Wink (tr). **26–27 Corbis:** Gregor Schuster (background). **Archivio Piaggio. 27 Alamy Images:** Norman Pogson (tr). **28–29 Alamy Images:** Bob Barnes (pebbles); Realimage. **29 Alamy Images:** Powered by Light / Alan Spencer (tc). **Corbis:** Galen Rowell (tr). **30–31 DAF Trucks N.V. 31 Getty Images:** China Foto Press (cr, br). **32 Corbis:** Reuters (br). **Getty Images:** MCT (bl). **32–33 Alamy Images:** Transtock Inc.. **33 Alamy Images:** Alex Segre (bl). **Truth About Trucking, LLC courtesy Allen Smith aka "AskTheTrucker":** (br). **34–35 Freightliner LLC. 35 Alamy Images:** Greg Balfour Evans (tr). **DAF Trucks N.V.:** (tc). **36–37 Daimler AG. 37 Alamy Images:** Gaspar R Avila (tr). **Corbis:** Construction Photography (tc). **38 Alamy Images:** imagebroker (b). **38–39 Alamy Images:** Dan Callister. **39 Camera Press:** Photo by Graham Turner / Guardian (t). **Corbis:** Hulton-Deutsch Collection (br); **Ocean** (bl). **40–41 Transporter. 41 Getty Images:** for NASCAR (b). **42 Alamy Images:** Coyote-Photography.co. uk / Shaun Finch (c). **42–43 Alamy Images:** Justin Kase zsixz (t); Naude / Dave J. Smith (b). **43 Jungheinrich:** (br). **SCHOPF Maschinenbau GmbH:** (tr, c). **44–45 Alamy Images:** Transtock Inc.. **46–47 fotoLibra :** Mike Sleigh. **47 Alamy Images:** pbpgalleries (tr); Transport Lesley (tc). **48 Knoxville News Sentinel:** Michael Patrick (t). **48–49 Alamy Images:** Giuseppe Masci. **49 Alamy Images:** nobleIMAGES (t); Gary Whitton (c); Transport / Mark Beton (b). **50 Alamy Images:** Navy Nhum (bc). **Corbis:** Reuters (br). **Mack Trucks Inc.:** (bl). **50–51 Corbis:** Richard Cummins. **51 Alamy Images:** ClassicStock (c); Mark Richardson (bl); Tim Scrivener (br); G&D Images (t). **52 Getty Images:** (tr). **52–53 Corbis:** Icon SMI / David J. Griffin. **54–55 Newmar Corporation. 55 Alamy Images:** David Chedgy (tr); pbpgalleries (tc). **56 Alamy Images:** Alvey & Towers Picture Library (tr); Chris Cooper-Smith (cl); imagebroker (bl). **56–57 Alamy Images:** Transtock Inc. (t). **Marchi Mobile GmbH:** (b). **57 Just Go (www.justgo. uk.com).** : (tr). **58–59 Corbis:** EPA. **59 Getty Images:** (tr, tc). **60 Caters News Agency:** Roger Snider (c, br, bl). **60–61 Caters News Agency:** Roger Snider (t). **61 Alamy Images:** vario images GmbH & Co KG (br). **62 Alamy Images:** PCN Photography (b). **Corbis:** NewSport / Alan Ashley (t). **63 Alamy Images:** Ian Dagnall (c); ZUMA Press, Inc. (t); Michael Doolittle (bl); Gunter Nezhoda (br). **64–65 Corbis:** George Disario. **66–67 Larry Crum:** IHRA Photo. **67 Alamy Images:** AlamyCelebrity. **68–69 SuperStock:** Tips Images. **69 Kenworth Australia:** photo by Voss Photography (tc, tr). **70 Alamy Images:** Joanne Moyes (tl); Henryk Sadura (tr). **70–71 Corbis:** Richard T. Nowitz. **71 Corbis:** Karen Kasmauski (tr). **The Cowles Center for Dance & the Performing Arts and Artspace Projects, Minneapolis, MN.:** (c). **72–73 Getty Images:** Bloomberg. **73 Carpat Belaz Group (www.belaz-mining.com):** (tr). **Corbis:** Douglas Keister (tc). **74–75 Mammoet Holding B.V. 75 Alamy Images:** Greenshoots Communications (cb). **Getty Images:** Gallo Images (t). **Leighton Asia:** (br). **SuperStock:** imagebroker (ca). **76–77 Foremost Industries LP. 77 Alamy Images:** Danita Delimont (tr). **Arctic Trucks:** photo by Gísli Jónsson (cr). **78 Corbis:** DPA (b). **Getty Images:** AFP (cl). **78–79 Getty Images:** Stocktrek Images (c). **79 Alamy Images:** Matthew Richardson (cr). **Corbis:** Reuters / Rebecca Cook / Handout (br). **Getty Images:** (tr). **80–81 Daimler AG. 81 Alamy Images:** Mark Scheuern (br). **Siyamak Rouhi Dehkordi:** (cr). **82 Corbis:** Gene Blevins / LA Daily News (tc). **Getty Images:** Stocktrek Images (tl). **82–83 Corbis:** Reuters. **83 Getty Images:** (tl). **NASA:** (ca). **84 Alamy Images:** Green Stock Media (bc). **Getty Images:** AFP (br). **84–85 Corbis:** Car Culture. **86 Alamy Images:** Sherab (tr). **Corbis:** (bl). **Fotolia:** AVD (tl). **86–87 Corbis:** Science Faction / U.S. Navy – digital version copy (b). **87 Alamy Images:** Flake (tl). SuperStock: imagebroker (tr). **88 Gibbs Technologies:** (tl, tr). **88–89 Gibbs Technologies. 89 Getty Images:** AFP (c). **Gibbs Technologies:** (tl). **90 Getty Images:** AFP (cl). **90–91 Volvo Truck Corporation. 96 Daimler AG**

All other images © Dorling Kindersley
For further information see:
www.dkimages.com